Anna's Corn

For Michael, Laura, Beth, Chad,
and all who love the corn.
— *B. S.*

I dedicate this book in memory of my parents,
Dr. Samuel Michael and Zita Bloom.
— *L. J. B.*

Text ©2002 by Barbara Santucci
Illustrations ©2002 by Lloyd Bloom
Published 2002 by Eerdmans Books for Young Readers
An imprint of Wm. B. Eerdmans Publishing Company
255 Jefferson S.E.,Grand Rapids, Michigan 49503
P.O. Box 163, Cambridge CB3 9PU U.K.

Printed in Hong Kong

02 03 04 05 06 07 08 7 6 5 4 3 2 1

Library of Congress Cataloging-in-Publication Data
Santucci, Barbara.
Anna's Corn / by Barbara Santucci ; illustrated by Lloyd Bloom.
p. cm.
Summary: Anna is reluctant to plant the kernels of corn her grandpa has left her upon his death,
until she realized that the act will help her remember the times they listened to the music of the
corn together.
ISBN 0-8028-5119-3 (cloth : alk. paper)
[1. Grandfathers—Fiction. 2. Death—Fiction. 3. Corn—Fiction.]
I. Bloom, Lloyd, ill. II. Title.
PZ7.S23863An 1997
[E]— dc21

96-51151
CIP
AC

The illustrations were created in water-soluble colored pencil
and graphite and soft pastel.
The display type was set in Casablanca Antique.
The text type was set in Caslon 224.

Anna's Corn

Written by **Barbara Santucci**

Illustrated by **Lloyd Bloom**

Eerdmans Books for Young Readers

Grand Rapids, Michigan   Cambridge, U. K.

Anna and Grandpa walked down the gravel road from the farmhouse to the cornfield. Autumn leaves swirled around their feet. Anna's walking stick matched the tap-step pace of Grandpa's cane.

"Listen to the corn, Anna," Grandpa said. "It makes its own kind of music."

"That's silly, Grandpa. Corn doesn't make music."

"Oh, yes, it does. But the wind has to be just right."

When they reached the field, Grandpa set his cane down.
"Cup your hand behind your ear, like this," he said, showing
Anna. "And be very still."

Anna pulled herself up tall and stood as still as the
scarecrow staked in the field. She cupped her hand behind
her ear like Grandpa had shown her.

"I hear the wind," she said. "But I don't hear the music."

"Be patient, Anna."

As they stood side by side, a sudden gust of wind breathed
through the dried corn stalks. Anna heard a whisper that grew
until a song formed. A raspy song, like Grandpa's voice.

"I hear it!" Anna shouted. "It crackles just like you."

Grandpa laughed and hugged her close to him. Then he reached over and snapped a cob from its stalk. He peeled the husk back, picked off a few kernels, and handed them to Anna.

"These are for you to plant next spring. You can store them in my leather pouch until then." He loosened the strings of the little pouch he took out of his pocket.

"Will they be my corn, Grandpa?" Anna asked, dropping the seeds one by one into the pouch.

"Yes, they will be Anna's corn."

Anna took Grandpa's hand as they
made their way back to the farmhouse.

That winter, Grandpa grew weaker and weaker until he could no longer walk, not even with his cane. He spent most of his time in bed, and Anna sat with him whenever she could.

"Promise me you'll plant your seeds next spring, Anna," Grandpa said one night. "Even if I can't go with you." He spoke so softly that Anna could hardly hear the crackle in his voice.

"I promise, Grandpa. We'll drive you down to the field so you can watch."

But soon after Anna made her promise, Grandpa died.

Anna felt very sad. She missed everything about Grandpa — his smile, the smell of his overalls, his voice. For many nights she cried herself to sleep with the leather pouch tucked under her pillow.

Anna often took the seeds out of the pouch and felt their hardness in her hands. Sometimes she felt hard inside. And empty too, like the cornfields lying beneath the winter snow and ice. She remembered Grandpa and the promise. She wondered if she would ever hear the corn's music again.

When May arrived and apple blossoms laced the backyard trees, Anna and Mama planted corn in the field.

They worked day after day until the sun set. But Anna
didn't plant her corn.

One night as she tucked Anna into bed, Mama asked, "Why don't you plant the seeds Grandpa gave you?"

"I like them just the way they are," Anna answered.

"They'll never become corn unless you plant them."

"If I bury them, they'll be gone forever."

Mama smoothed Anna's hair back from her forehead. "They won't be gone, Anna. They'll just be different. We'll take care of them, and with the help of the sun and the rain your seeds will grow into beautiful corn."

"But will I be able to hear the music again, like I did with Grandpa?"

"If you don't plant them, you never will."

After her mother left the room, Anna lay in bed thinking. She reached under her pillow where she kept Grandpa's pouch. She took out the seeds and cradled them in her hand before dropping off to sleep.

The next morning, when she was having breakfast with Mama, Anna placed the leather pouch on the table between them.

"I'm going to plant my seeds this morning," she announced.

"I'm glad, Anna."

After breakfast, Anna and her mother walked out to the field and planted Anna's corn seeds next to some of the little green shoots that had already begun to sprout. They marked the seeds with a sign that said *ANNA'S CORN*.

Every day they checked to see if Anna's seeds had sprouted through the soft dirt.

One morning Anna spotted the tiny green shoots popping up. "Look, Mama!"

Her mother smiled. "Pretty soon they'll be taller than you, Anna."

The stalks of corn grew all that summer. And every day Anna listened for their song.

By July the corn reached Anna's knees. She listened to
the rain pit-patting against the young plants.

By August the corn towered above Anna's head, shadowing her from the blistering sun that sizzled down. She heard the wind rush-rushing through the stalks. But it wasn't the corn's full song.

By October the corn was ready to harvest. One cool, gusty day, Anna walked to the field alone. She snapped one of her cobs from its stalk, then peeled the husk back and picked a few kernels.

"I'll plant these new seeds next spring," said Anna as she put them inside Grandpa's leather pouch.

A sudden breeze sighed across the field.

Anna pulled herself up tall and stood as still as the scarecrow guarding the field. She cupped her hand behind her ear like Grandpa had shown her. Listening. Listening to the corn.

Its whisper grew louder and stronger until, at last, a song formed on the wind. A song she knew. A raspy song. The song she had shared with Grandpa.